They Never Wanted Me to Wake Up to My Anointing

Yvette Roland

Fulton Books
Meadville, PA

Published by Fulton Books 2025

ISBN 979-8-89221-204-5 (paperback)
ISBN 979-8-89221-205-2 (digital)

Printed in the United States of America

This is my life story.

Hello to all, my name is Yvette Roland, and I was born on April 16, 1970. I am dedicating this book to my Father, Jesus Christ, my God, and my father, Clifton Gene Roland. I am very grateful for all the challenges that I have experienced in my life. I can say that now because, of course, I understand the whole picture of my destiny now. Well, I am figuring it out every day, and I am truly grateful for God for revealing this to me. He is my strength and motivator in my life. I know my story might seem unreal, but here it is, and I am going for it.

It all began when I was created. My dad used to say jokingly, "Yvette was conceived when the man was walking on the moon." Sometimes he would say I was an accident because my mom forgot to take her birth control pill. I never thought anything negative of what my dad used to say. I did learn later in life that God makes no accidents.

I was born to my father, Clifton Gene Roland, and my mother, Maria Francis Roland. I was born in Long Beach, California, on a naval base. My dad was in the navy. I lived a lot of my youth at navy bases across the United States. I can generally say I had a normal childhood. I was happy.

I did draw closer to my father in my life than my mother. I felt more love from him than my mom for some reason. My dad was in the navy for twenty years. My father was absent for long periods of time because he would be out to sea for many months at one time. I had a sister named Rosemary and a brother named Troy.

As a child, I had a fear of sleeping by myself for some reason. I can't recall why, but I know there is a sufficient reason. I know I will find the truth to why soon. I never really thought that it was something more than just being scared to sleep by myself. I know it was something more. I just feel it in my soul and spirit.

I am also going to talk about spiritual warfare. I was raised as Catholic but didn't know anything about the Bible. My mother was from Panama, and my dad was an orphan at an Oklahoma nun orphanage from two years old to seventeen years old when he joined the service of the navy. While he was overseas, he met my mother. He said she was the most beautiful woman he had ever met. I have a picture of my mom and dad when they were young. He looked very happy but not so much like my mom. That is just the way I see it. Anyways, she got pregnant with my brother, and my dad married her and moved to California, where he was stationed. My dad volunteered to go to Vietnam to fight in the war.

My early childhood memories are very empty, like erased. I cannot remember a lot of it, but it was just like crying at their door when my parents would not let me sleep with them. I believe there was something else to this. It's pretty clear that they wiped something from my memory when I was a child. I sit and try to remember. I can remember my mom saying that I had to be put on some type of braces for my back and legs. Later in life, when I was in the eighth grade getting a physical, I didn't pass because I had a curvature of the spine, and I had to go and get pictures done and X-rays on my back when I was a kid. I believe because I am RH negative, I have an extra vertebra. This is what I believe RH negative people have. Of course, no one told me anything about my extra vertebra. They said I had scoliosis of the spine.

I know that this is a journey in life of mistakes that I have made in the present and past, and God is rewriting my story that was put in my head of how it is supposed to be. God said, "No, this is how it is going to be." Pretty much I was hidden in plain sight. I wasn't even aware that I had been chosen. Anytime I made a prediction and it came true, no one would ever say, "Wow, Yvette, you were right about that." Naw, to tell you the truth, they *never wanted me to wake up* to who I really am. That's the truth.

I am just now, as the last two years, reliving all my past traumatic memories of how the plan of the devil, the enemy, had hijacked so many people, family, friends, lovers, body, and soul to come against me. The enemy had a plan for me to be bitter, hateful, in a terrible, unloving type of atmosphere. Maybe I have been like that from all the black magic, voodoo, and spiritual warfare—I didn't know any better. Now I am fully aware of the tricks of the devil, and I have forgiven, and I thank my enemies for helping me to be the spiritual healer I am today. I'm kind of going through different stages in my life of reflection of all the memories—good, bad, traumatic—and indifferent emotions that I have gone through. I am inputting my story to the best of my abilities as to what has happened to me in my life.

I can remember as a young child to not lie to God. I was tested as a child by my siblings when I was caught doing something that was very shameful. My brother asked me, and I lied. Then he said, "Get the Bible and put your hand on the Bible and swear." I could not do it because I *feared* the Lord. I still can remember that day as if it just happened.

I know that we are on this planet to evolve and be our brother's keeper and help one another. This is not what is truly going on. I know there are good people in this world because I have come across many who are earth angels to help me evolve to who I truly am and why I am here.

The illusions that were engraved in my head were a lie.

I struggled with abandonment issues when my mother and father were separated from one another, and I had to fly on a plane by myself when I was young to visit my dad in Texas and then live with my mom for the rest of the time.

I felt it was a hardening trauma time in my life because of the separation of my parents. I felt unloved, unliked, and indifferent in my spirit and soul. I felt as if I was torn apart in my heart. I would cry leaving my mom and then be happy to see my dad, then cry leaving my dad and coming back to stay with my mom.

I know that this was only to make me stronger, but at the time, I didn't know any better because I was young. I thought this was just my life and everybody goes through this as a child. I want to say that this left me lonely and very unsure of myself and my happiness. It made me very sad and alone when they were apart.

This trauma stayed with me throughout my life and led to addictions—addictions in love and lust—and codependences of relations.

I was not the type to go to church every Sunday, but I did have a personal relationship with God and prayed and felt that there was hope in this world for better even though I was hurting inside.

When I was a teenager, I fell in love and had sex. Unfortunately, I was never taught anything about the birds and the bees. When my period started, I didn't even know what the heck was going on with me. I was in a family with my mom and dad but was never taught about life. I thought I was on top of the world.

During this time, I was also introduced to hard drugs, like crack cocaine, snorting coke, methamphetamine, etc. The crack cocaine started to become my love, the one that I would go to or think about all the time. It liked to control of my whole being, and I couldn't stop. I went to several rehabs. I would go for my family, friends, relationships, or court. I never really went to rehab for myself; it was always for family, loved ones, court, etc. It was something I wanted to do, but I knew in the long run, it was something that I needed to evolve to succeed in life, or I was going to die, go to jail, or get addicted to horrible misfortunes in life. I was a hardhead and continually went through the cycles repeatedly. Not really understanding this stronghold of addiction over me, but I recognize it today, and I thank God for the revelations that he has given me about this.

The best thing is that my addictions are no longer my strongholds or toxic behaviors because God released that nasty demonic force of addictions off me when I started tapping in and praying to God for answers and love. He revealed the reasons and evacuated those demons that had me under a demonic spell. Praise God from whom our blessings flow.

I am now fifty-two years old and have been on this journey, and within the last two years really, I have been diving down deep within my soul, spirit, and the universe of what the heck and who the heck I am.

When I started tapping into the divine for questions, I felt an overwhelming, beautiful, warm feeling all over my body, and I knew it was God. I was so happy; it was like the best day of my life. I want to share this with the world on how to fight these demonic strongholds on our families and curses that have been placed on our families battling with generational curses. I never knew anything about spirituality. I always had a relationship with God but never knew about tapping in, meditating, going through spiritual life paths, knowing what we speak out of our mouth becomes, and receiving gifts from people could be cursed (for instance, clothes, shoes, or anything).

A lot of times, we just think that the family we were born into is our family. This is not correct. You see, God made us in his image and had already written our destiny before we were even created. I know I was chosen to help humanity and that this is what I am going to do. I trust the Lord to guide me in all my steps toward fulfilling my destiny.

It seemed like to me that when I was a child, I couldn't quite become who I was truly in my God's eyes, Jesus Christ. I knew that this place, earth, was beautiful, but there was also a lot of darkness.

When I was in the third grade in the '70s, my father took the whole family to a drive-in movie to watch *The Exorcist*. Let me tell you that after that show, I could not sleep by myself. It put a lot of fear in my spirit. I don't believe that my father thought it wouldn't have a big effect on me. Well, that night, I fell asleep right when they were putting a needle in her neck. This movie entered my home, and I watched its entirety, and that was when the *fear* of being by myself creeped in or sleeping by myself intensified.

I watched a lot of scary movies as a child and was scared but curious. I think the more you are exposed to these demonic movies, the more you conform to this reality that the Hollywood filmmakers' demonic vessels are pushing toward the public. This is a way of conditioning us as a human race to get ready for the king of *all* lies. Amen.

Of course, at that time, I had no idea. I am pretty sure that most of the public also felt that it wasn't that big of a deal. Understanding the time we are in right now, it all makes sense. I am just grateful to God for allowing my enemies to do what they did to me because now I am who I am today. We must stay grateful in all times of our lives. I now believe I know this to be true because I have been spiritually attacked and manipulated all my life from when I was born. The best thing about it was God was fighting all these battles when I was not aware of who I was. By his grace, love, and mercy for me (us), we must understand it's not about us; it's about Jesus Christ, God. We all are children of God, and the enemy is doing everything in his power to *kill us*. It took many years before I truly understood my destiny. I am still learning every day, and this is something I want to share with everyone.

My father died on October 28, 2013, and it was one of the most devasting times in my life. I went through an emotional breakdown and was so sad and depressed after his death. It felt like my best friend, the only one that was ever in my corner, just left and was gone. I was broken, and I found out my ex had been molesting my oldest daughter for years. I wanted to die. I was doing drugs every night crying; *I was* in one of the darkest times in my life. I didn't think I would ever get out of it. God had a different plan for me and wouldn't let me die.

During this time, I kept waking up at 3:33 a.m. I didn't know it was God trying to speak with me. I knew nothing about spirituality. This went on for years until around 2019, and then 2020 hit, and I started looking at my life different.

Basically, it was when the pandemic happened. You see, the enemy thought this was going to keep us farther away from God and us connecting. Anything that the enemy wanted to do bad to us, God will use it for his good and our good. Praise God!

I got a couple of good jobs, one with census. After that was done, I applied for a billing and coding job. I was able to get hired, and I was so anxious to learn. I had gone to school much earlier in life for billing and coding, but right before I was like points or so for the associate degree, my dad got ALS. I stopped going.

I got this job and was working from home. I was learning, but God didn't want me there. I had a bigger mission, and when the 2020 election came, my goodness, it felt like darkness was yelling out loud on the TV screen. After two years of that job, I was let go, and I was actually grateful and told them I felt like there was a calling for me to do something amazing in my life. I claimed it right there in front of HR and the supervisor, not even knowing what it was.

I sit here and reflect of all the events in my life and how it has led me to here, and I am so grateful and always say how grateful I am to my God Jesus Christ to work through me to help humanity.

After that happened, I had more time to myself and received unemployment. I just stayed busy around the house and nature outside by watering my flowers and grass to keep them green. One day, I was thinking to myself and wondering, *How come my life is like this?* I have been doing a lot better, staying at home, stopped my crack addiction, sex, feeling sad because I was rejected, and all the nasty things that the enemy wants us to feel about ourselves. I just looked up at the sky and cried to God, and that was when everything changed. I felt a warm feeling upon my face, and I knew God was there. I started to cry and weep, and I was so grateful that he was listening. I no longer felt alone. I knew something was with me. I felt empowered to know more about my life.

I started praying. I got into the Bible. I also got into different spiritual practices to broaden my understanding of the universe. Everything we have was given to us by God for *free*. Everyone should know this. This lie that we have electric companies, phone companies, water companies, taxes, and all that stuff they are claiming, it's enslaving us to this fake reality. They want to keep us in that mindset of always having to pay for shit. Okay. It's a scam, and they are caught. The time we are living in is going back to the beginning right now.

I want to talk about spiritual warfare and how to recognize that you are in some type of spiritual warfare. If you are addicted to drugs, alcohol, has depression, anxiety, is suicidal, etc., that is a spiritual warfare. Once you recognize that this is what it is, you are headed in the right direction. These dark, demonic, soulless vessels that are being used to fool and trick us are coming to an end. They have been using Hollywood movies to conform us into their sick agenda. We have been going right along with it. Listen, no longer can they lie to us. It is written their time is up. Now let's pray for the coming of Jesus Christ to save us, and let me tell you, he's coming. I will have more information on how exactly I have been fighting these demonic demons in my life.

Praise be to God for all his love for us. Now if you have not turned your life over to Jesus Christ, say now, ask God to come into your life and be your Lord and Savior. Repent of your sins, and sin no longer, amen. You're one of God's children, and he loves us all praise. God, I love you, I'm not ever giving up on my life. I love God, and I am working for him and only him.

*****

I can remember traveling as a child when I was young to different navy bases. I never stayed in one place long enough to really develop any childhood friends for more than maybe five years to where I would move again. I really thought about the intensity of never letting me stay in one environment where I could connect with friendship and with myself, to truly be myself and know and love myself. It was very dysfunctional to the sense of not belonging somewhere and always moving and having to start over on friendships and locations. I hope that makes sense.

I did have many good childhood memories though. I can remember when I first started driving a car, my window was down, and I was like maybe fourteen or fifteen. I was probably going around twenty miles an hour when all of a sudden, something flew in my window. I stopped at my uncle Rayburn's house, which was right around the corner, and he got out a baby owl. I know today I have some kind of connection with birds. When I started to notice that the world wasn't what we were programmed to believe, everything changed in my life.

In 2022, for about a month, I started seeing black birds, ravens, or crows. Several of them every day for like a month started circling in the sky above my house. I was like, "What the heck is going on?" My oldest daughter, Meghan, also witnessed this; it was like "What is really going on?" I was looking for answers and, of course, headed to the internet with questions and the Bible. I was intrigued by what was the universe trying to tell me. I have been living in the same house for fifteen-plus years, and this had never happened to me before. There were ravens and black birds coming to the trees in my yard every day, yack-kack-kacking at me. There was this one black bird that was huge, and my daughter Emily was like, "Wow, he looks like Jeepers Creepers."

*****

I was raised a Catholic but had no relationship with Catholic people. I didn't even comprehend what was going on in this church. I knew to get on my knees when I was told and stuff like that. One thing I can say for certain is that I *feared God*. It was instilled in my soul from an early age.

I would read my horoscope but never really believed in witchcraft. I was always told tarot cards are from the devil. I learned it's your intentions on what you're doing with them. For some reason, this lady on YouTube came up on my feed. What drew me to her was that she had a picture of a raven in the background of her platform. She stated she used reading cards for money or other purposes, but she now read cards for the light. So I started briefly watching, expanding my consciousness of my reality and what was really going on in this world. It seemed that after COVID-19 lockdowns and the Biden administration, it seemed apparent that there was something else that was going on in this world that I was stepping into. You see, as a child, I used to ask my dad so many questions about this and that and what that means and so on. So I am the type of person who seeks out the truth.

I accidentally left my TV on when I fell asleep one night, and I woke up around three in the morning to use the restroom, and while I was walking to the restroom, I heard my name, Yvette, clear as day coming from the TV. I was like, "What?" I had been asking God to give me some kind clarity in my life that maybe what I am thinking or feeling was true. Right then, I knew the Holy Spirit was like, "Yvette, yes." I couldn't believe it.

Now my name is not a common name, Yvette. For that one split second waking up in the middle of the night and hearing my name as clear as a bell, I was floored. I was shocked, happy, gracious, blessed, and grateful that the Holy Spirit was listening to me. I was like, "Okay, God, you got my attention." It was like the Holy Spirit was listening to everything I was saying, feeling, crying about, and trying to understand, and just right then, it was "Okay, God, you got my attention." That was beautiful. Some people would say, "Oh, that was just a coincidence." All I can say is that there are no coincidences in life. Once you start realizing that there are no coincidences in this life, that is when your life starts.

I started diving into history as much as I could. Then one day, on my YouTube feed, a man named Franchot Pearson showed up, and I knew it was from God because he taught me about the five principles and the five seeds. I didn't know anything. I was so interested. He informed me that the devil, Satan, or whatever you want to call it, the dark powers on this earth, must inform us before doing anything on this earth. The five seeds are colors, numbers, codes, calculation of time, and conclusions. I learned numerology and gematria from watching him and how to see beyond what was just being said. It was amazing, and I am still grateful to him for opening my eyes to what was really going on in this world. I knew that Mr. Pearson was put on my feed from God Jesus Christ. I was truly grateful of all the new information. It was like a whole new perspective of what the heck was going on this beautiful earth. I have to say that writing a book was something I never, in my life, thought would happen.

I started diving into my birth date, my life path number, and more. This was when I discovered who I am and that I am a child of God. I can remember when I started discovering all the numerology and life path that I was a life path one, which is me. I am an Aries, which is the first of the zodiac signs. It made sense then that I started looking up people closest to me and found out that my oldest daughter was a master key 33/6, my second daughter, Emily, was a life path eleven, Dad was a twenty-two, and someone I was dating off and on was a 33/6. I looked all that up and found out they are ascended masters here to help me on my destiny. Praise God.

I went back to my birth date and looked again and noticed that I am a one, but it was a ten. I was floored and started crying and asked God, "Really? Me…" I grabbed my Bible and just flipped to any page asking God what does this mean, and it went right to Isaiah 44, 45. I started praying and crying to God, thanking him, and right then, I got on my knees and thanked him for loving me and entrusting me for this task. I was in a state of excitement and love for our Father who loves us unconditionally.

I was amazed how this was happening to me. I was a drug addict, had failed relationships in love, friends, and family. I was so grateful for his loving mercy on my life. I never knew this until last year. I thanked God for that COVID-19 lockdown. This was when I started my journey with knowing that God has a special mission plan in my life. I was so excited and started telling my family how I felt the presence of God came to me and touch me to let me know that he loves me and I was going to succeed in my life.

My family was not accepting of my anointing or that I was chosen. It was like a slap in my face because I couldn't understand why the people in my life who were my family could not be excited for this good news. It really made me think about the people around me and what was really going on.

I turned my back on the people, drugs, and places and started really tapping into my spirituality. I would be outside meditating and thanking God aloud outside and praising him for his love for me. I was in a beautiful state of knowing I am not alone in this world like I thought I was. God just filled me up with an endless amount of love. I never thought I could have a relationship like this or that I was chosen. I have always been like the black sheep of the family, a free spirit, kind like a gypsy. My mom used to tell me I lived me life like a gypsy in my younger years. I believe she knew some kind of truth to that.

Growing up as a child, I can remember going to school and teachers would tell me that I was spelling my name wrong. They would tell me to write my name like Ivette. Then I would start writing my name for that year like that. Then on my first grade, they said, "No, you spell your name like Evette." Then I would be writing my name like that. In all actuality, it was like programming me to change who I was. I didn't know; I was just a kid.

Throughout my years in school, my dad was in the navy, and I never stayed at one location very long. We would get transferred to different locations of navy bases to live. It was hard to have a friendship with anyone for very long.

I can remember being best friends in elementary school with a triplets. This was nothing I thought was different, but now thinking about it, I have never met triplets since then.

I can remember when I was young, I did something to my sister's water pick. She had some little cups, and I got one of those little cups and urinated in it just to see if I could stand and pee. Silly but I did and poured it out, but I guess I did not clean it good enough. I came home from playing outside one day and got confronted by my brother in front of the whole family, asking if I had done that. I was in the fifth grade and was embarrassed 'cause my brother was laughing at me and yelling loudly. I said no. He immediately grabbed the Bible and said, "Yvette, put your hand on the Bible and say you didn't pee in the cup." I could not. I knew that I couldn't lie to God. They all started laughing at me because I couldn't lie to God. I feared God even at that age.

I can remember also my brother forcing me to smoke weed in his room, and I would be crying, not wanting to do it, and he would be laughing, making fun of me but forcing me to do it. Then since I had to do it, I would be crying and he would laugh. Now it seemed like he forgot.

As time went on, my dad and mother separated, and my dad moved to Texas from Florida. I would travel on the plane to visit my dad for Christmas, crying because I was leaving my mom. Then I would see my dad and then cry leaving my dad. One day, I decided that I wanted to live with my dad, and so I did.

I moved to Texas from Pensacola, Florida, and lived with my dad. Eventually, my mom moved from Florida to be with my dad. They reconciled, and my sister came too.

During high school, I was like any other kid. Around the tenth grade, me and my best friend basically got a new best friend, and I was crushed; it was like a breakup from a loved one. I was devastated. I grew modestly, and we were not rich, but her new best friend was. I was very hurt and lonely. This was the time I started meeting boys. I had a boyfriend, and I was in love. He introduced me to crack cocaine, methamphetamine, and marijuana. This rejection of my best friend was all orchestrated by the enemy to make me feel like there was something wrong with me. It was witchcraft, dark arts. This was the way the enemy wanted to keep me in a low, depressing state of mind, like I was not a good friend, lover, girlfriend, sister. You name it, I was called it. Especially in high school with the crack epidemic started and that song "Dear Yvette," let me tell you, I was even out there yet, but that song had a way to look at me in a disgusting way, and it played out during my life with other ex-relationships. I see all that now. I feel like my whole life was like *The Truman Show* literally.

I didn't realize at the time that all these hard drugs were also a form of witchcraft.

(We are *chosen*…will always be protected. Don't forget, and we are targeted! Put your armor of God on everywhere you go in and out of your house. Ask for hedge of protection around your house, children, animals, loved ones, destiny, bloodline. Always give thanks and love to God Jesus Christ, the universe. He loves everyone, waiting for humanity to call to him; he's here. I love you, God, amen. Let's go! I love everyone! Peace be with everyone!) This was a post I did on YouTube on January 23, 2023. Now back to the book.

I realized that all my disappointments in my life was not about me; it was about Jesus Christ who is in all of us. I realize that now, but then I had no clue we all have within us that God put in each human being on this earth. We have been programmed a certain way to think, feel what is right or wrong, what makes us special or with anything—wealth, status, marriage—who is the first one to get this or that, or how many people liked my video and how many followings I have. It's not about that; we have been in an illusion for so long.

I fell in love during high school and basically became codependent on that love for everything. When I got rejected from him, I was crushed and turned to drugs and not the Lord. This continued in my life. I would get a job and stay a while, but it wouldn't last. I had my first daughter in 1994. I didn't know anything about babies when Meghan was born. I just knew that I loved her so much; when I saw her, I became in love again. I knew she was an angel sent from heaven for me. I was thankful to God for letting her come into my existence.

When I had her and looked at her, it was like the most perfect love, and she was all mine. I never wanted to put her down. My in-laws were like "You hold her too much" and this and that. I listened and started on my drugs again because I never healed from the past afflictions that been stored up and wasn't praying and changing what I was doing. I was still using, and eventually, my daughter was taken from me from her dad. He got into another relationship and hid my daughter from me. I called the police, and they told me that possession was nine-tenths of the law. Since we never went to court, he had the right as a father to do this. I went into a rage of disbelief and that I wasn't worth of even living.

I started heavily doing drugs, staying away from my house for months at a time. Eventually, I sold my vehicle and walked the street for money to support my habits. Until one night at three in the morning, I looked up at the sky and cried out to God to help me. It wasn't an hour later that I got arrested. That was God saving my life. I didn't know that at that time, but that's what I know happened. By the grace of our Lord and Savior, he intervened in my life and saved me from myself. I thanked him, but I went to jail, got out, and did it again. You see, I was a knucklehead.

I went to several rehabs during my years of living, trying every AA, AN, sponsor, rehabs, lockdowns, and prison. But nothing worked until I surrendered to God, and by his grace and love for me, it's when I finally found myself and loved myself again. I had to go through all the trials and tribulations and wilderness and finally get to where I am today. I am so thankful to God for saving my life so many times.

March 27, 2023

I haven't written anything in a while. I had to move from my house I had been in since 2005. I just moved into a town house with my daughter Christina, who was fifteen. She was pregnant with my first grandson and was due to have Emmanuel in May. I'm excited and very proud that it's a boy and my first grandson.

I want to go back about one year ago when I had my encounter with God and felt his beautiful presence with him when I cried out to him at my old house. It was something so beautiful, and I felt his warmth around my body. It was beautiful and something that was instant, and I knew it was the Holy Spirit. That was when everything changed in my life. God has been revealing who I am and that I have a mission here to help humanity. I am here to shine a light on the darkness in this world. The message is that God loves us and want us to call out to him and ask him to be the author in our life on all activities that we do during the day. He wants to be in our lives and help us. We have been tricked by the devil, dark entities that are roaming this earth.

I'm writing this on behalf of my Lord Jesus Christ as my testimony that God is alive and here with us and loves each and every one of us.

Also, I want to mention that during my first pregnancy, I had to get a shot during my seventh month called a RHOGRAM shot so my baby will survive. I never really dug into it any further than I am RH-. My blood type is RH-, A-. I researched that RH- is a rare blood. I have also realized that I am chosen, one of the 144,000 just like it was stated in the Bible.

We need to wake up, and I can help you wake up. If you want to wake up to who you are, then pick up the Bible and repent, state that God is your Lord and Savior, and ask him to come into your life. It doesn't matter how, who, what you have done or are doing, just come as you are. He loves you, and I love you too. Amen.

April 04, 2023

I am writing again so I can put it on paper. I just want to put down that I never knew that God was with me all along during all my life. I knew he existed, and I did pray, but because of how the enemy had me, I never felt like I was good enough to pray, to go to him and ask him for anything. I felt so ashamed and rejected, depressed, and hopeless at times. I would lose everything and relapse and just could not understand why I couldn't seem to succeed in life, love, and career. This is how the enemy wants us to feel and be like, which is all a *lie*.

I want to talk about right now how I am so grateful for God's precious love for me. I love you, God, so much. I am very grateful of how my God has opened my eyes to what is really going on in this world, and it's nothing like this world wants us to believe it is.

I want to say.

May 30, 2023

I'm writing again. I have voice-recorded my life in the process also. I just want to say these to everyone. I am just a regular person; my hands have gotten dirty and have committed sins in my life. I am nowhere perfect. Only Jesus Christ is perfect. God wants me to record my story to help others, to let humanity know that God Jesus Christ, is alive and what he has done for me. I'm here to help others see the unseen in their lives and the steps I took to protect myself and my family (children) against the powers that are here in this world that are not of light.

I know the world or Hollywood portrays that things supernatural are just a conspiracy because they want us to remain blind to the truth. I'm here from God to tell humanity that we are children of God and he loves us, and we have been hoodwinked long enough. Amen. I want to help awaken people to their calling that God has programmed in you to do here. Believe I was in the matrix for fifty years, not even knowing that I was *chosen* as one of God's spiritual warriors, truth bearer. This is what I am here to proclaim and let the world know. I love everyone, and God bless you, amen.

July 30, 2023

I am deciding to journal my daily life activities. I noticed that I haven't talked about a lot of supernatural events that have occurred in my life that to this day, it was something supernatural: when I started my journey of waking up after the birds were circling my house for like a month. One day, my daughter came to me when we're at my old house and said, "Did you hear that?" I said yes, but I thought it was her in her room, but she said no, it was outside. We went outside, and the top part of a tree where I park my car just fell. I took a video and picture of it, but to me, it was a direct message from the devil, stating he was mad because I am no longer bowing down to his schemes of deception. I was a little frightened, but we took that part of the tree, and I put it on a burn pile to make a bomb fire.

It sat out there for a few months, and one day, when my oldest daughter came over, I was like "Let's light it and dance around like the Indians"; I was just playing. We lit it, and it was so high I had to turn on the water hose to bring the fire down. One of Meghan's friends was there and took a picture of it, and you could clearly see a dragon with my ex's head on it. I also have that picture. I told my mom about it and showed her, and she just opened her mouth, like wow, but another tree fell in the back, and my mom asked me to let the people cutting my yard haul it away. It made me feel she didn't want me to see what will come out of it; I told her no, that I'm going to keep it.

Another time, I was in the hospital and just got done getting my gallbladder removed, and I was in the hospital bed trying to sleep, but the bed kept moving every twenty minutes, so every time I was about to fall asleep, it would move. Finally, I dozed off, and in my dream state, I couldn't breathe, so I was trying to wake up, but I couldn't, then I opened my eyes, and when I did, this gray smoke shot straight up to the ceiling and went to the corner and then across the room to another corner and disappeared. That gray cloud entity was basically choking me. Needless to say, I checked myself out early from the hospital the next day.

Halloween 2022

I was at my old house by myself. I went to sleep early. God woke me up in the middle of the night. It was pitch black. I grabbed my phone to turn the light on and walked to the air conditioner controller in the other room and noticed it was not on, and I knew the power was off. I smiled and went back to my bed and started praying to God, and within a minute, the lights came back on. I hollered, "Thank you, God, I love you!"

In the morning, I went outside; and in one of my trees, my daughter Emily threw a Hula-Hoop in the tree, and it had been there for a few years. But this morning, it was on the ground and broken into pieces. So I don't know what kind of ritual or attack was aimed at me, but it failed because God was with me.

After that incident, there was more. My youngest daughter Christina had gotten a cat from one of her friends and hid it in the house from me for like two weeks before I found out. Christina was telling me that her friend couldn't keep it and she loved this cat. She was really working on my emotions, so I let it slide even though I didn't approve. There was something weird about this cat. My dog would always sleep in the bed with me. But when this cat was at my house, my dog slept in her doggy bed at the end of my bed, and she would guard me during my sleep from this cat. I would randomly hear her during the night barking and chasing this cat away from my room. One night, I was sleeping, and the spirit woke me up, and that cat was right beside me in the bed, and I hollered, and it ran. The other cats also didn't like that cat. I believe that cat was cloned. It eventually went outside and disappeared.

Also, during this time, I went to sleep, and I felt like someone was tapping gently on my lips. In my dream state, I woke up and pulled out a sword and cut the head off this demon that was fondling my body, my lips; it was awesome.

In another dream state, I was at my house, and it was dark, and I saw a van parked outside of my house at the beginning of the driveway, and it was my ex's father who was already dead with two other people just outside. Then I saw a truck pull up, and it was my ex, and then he came in my house and jumped, lying down on my couch like he was still living with me. I saw him and told him to "GET THE HELL OUT OF MY HOUSE." He looked at me in the dream state and left. I think he was shocked to see that I saw him in my dream. I was happy that I stood my ground to him and ordered him out immediately. I was grateful to God for showing me what he has been doing on with my spirit, soul.

Basically, I have had the government, elites, demons, demonic forces, family, lovers, friends, you name it, orchestrating my life and harvesting my energy for themselves.

The Holy Spirit wants me to mention when I met my X in the beginning of our relationship, I noticed he had a brand on the inside of his forearm with a circle with a star in it. I asked him what it was, and he stated it was a gang initiation when he was a juvenile. I believed him. This was a major red flag that I ignored. He told me he didn't believe in Jesus Christ as his lord and savior. Another Red flag.

At one time, when my ex lived with me, he told my oldest daughter that I was the crown and Meghan was the jewels on the crown and he was picking off the jewels. My ex also molested and raped my daughter Meghan. To this day, she is still healing from all the trauma that was inflicted on her. She's getting better. Praise God.

My father's *will* was changed on his deathbed by my brother and mother. I was told by my nephew and my great-aunt Joyce. I recently called my mom to get a copy of the will, and she put my brother on the phone and basically was acting like there was no will. Too bad I already got in touch with the lawyer and I had a copy of it today.

I don't hate anyone, but it was disappointing to know your whole life was manipulated by dark, demonic forces, and all the pain and suffering for fifty years was not in vain. This was my story, and I am putting it out here because these actions against me were wrong on so many levels. I know that my story is also someone else's story too. My understanding is that it is about dark versus light. I walked through hell and back a few times in my life, and I am still standing.

All the personal trials that I endured in life were very painful and dreadful. I want to say that there was a way, the truth, and the light. I just always knew in my heart that things would be better in my life no matter how hard they tried to make me feel like I was an outcast, the black sheep of the family. It was all a plan from when I was born. I am very grateful to God Jesus Christ for redeeming me and keeping me and for *waking me up*. Glory to God. I wake up every day thanking God for putting air in my lungs and giving me a chance at this beautiful life. Yes, I can say I have a beautiful life, and I am very grateful for all he has done for me. I dedicate my whole existence to the Almighty God my Creator. Amen

July 31, 2023

Also, at one time, when I was with my ex, we went to his friend's house and were outside, and all of a sudden, a macaw parrot came down flying from the tree to come right on my arm and landed. It was amazing. I was pregnant with my second child, and everyone was playing it off as if because I was pregnant that was why the bird landed on me. I didn't think so. I am very close to animals; it's like I can understand them to a certain extent. It's like a bond with them all the time. I have had animals saying "mom," baby horse smiling at me when I asked it to, and many more.

I also want to get on with numerology. My life path is ten or one. My home address, the numbers equaled nineteen, which is ten; my area code for my place of residence is 936. The loop around my town is loop 336, and the two digits in the middle of my Social Security number is sixty-nine. The building that is next to where I live is sixty-nine. The first phone number I got when I moved into the residence from 2005 until 2023 was the last four digits 3338. I am noticing so many synchronicities right in my life numbers from time, receipts, and whatever shape or form God wants me to see.

It's awesome to know that the universe is speaking to me and always around me in the name of Jesus Christ. Thank you, Abba Father.

August 01, 2023

God reminded me when I was twenty-two years old, I was with Meghan's Dad, my first child's dad. Except we didn't have Meghan yet. I was staying with him, and we were doing drugs and meth and living like gypsies. I can recall we were at this woman's house who we just moved into. I had been up for several days, and I was lying in my bed. I could hear Mike and his friends playing cards and stuff like that. I looked up to the ceiling, and I saw seven angels in white flying above me. I packed up my shit and moved back home to my parents' house. To me, it seemed like it was a warning sign to get out, so I did.

God was always with me during all the tribulations of my life, the ups and the downs. I believed in God, but I had felt that since I don't read the Bible, God didn't hear me. I felt like I had done way too much bad shit in my life, that I wasn't worthy to read the Bible because to me, that was so sacred. This is what the demonic forces had made me put out that illusion that I was too sinful to be worthy of his love or to even ask for anything, read the Bible, etc. It was all a *lie*. I am here as living proof that God does exist because I know him and he knows me. He loves me and everyone else. He makes us in his image and loves each and every one of us. He tells me to never stop praying and believing. Have faith as a mustard seed. Repent of your sins and sin no more. Ask him for help and guidance.

A lot of times right now we have so many demonic forces against us, and most of us cannot see. There are so many distractions in this world, but that is how Satan, devil, fallen angels, demons, and demonic forces want us to feel like. Especially working in a low vibration (sex, drugs, porn, homosexuality, immortality, envy, jealous), they just wants us to love money, sex, drugs, and power control. It is pretty disgusting, and they manipulate each and every one of us into believing that we are not the head but the tail. This is a lie, and I chop the heads off the snakes. I had to write something a little and smile because my life wasn't easy. I went through hell and back and hell again, and now I'm back better than ever in my life.

I know who I am, a chosen child of God. They never wanted me to wake up. My destiny is not with the devil. It never was. Until I started loving myself, reading the Bible, stop having sex, getting a relationship with God, eating better, exercising, loving on myself, stop doing hard drugs, meditating and saying positive affirmations, and being more positive about my life and listening more, and every day, I am learning more and more about who I am and what my life is. I am so grateful to God Jesus Christ.

Right now, we are in a spiritual war against demonic spirits, fallen angels, and demons.

August 07, 2023

I know that this reality is bullshit. I was watching this elder man on YouTube talking about maritime, seamen, manifestations, birth certificates. We are owned by the Rothschilds, Rockefeller, and English Banks. He spoke on the Phoenicians, and I learned about them from Franchot Pearson. They worshipped Baal and would sacrifice babies to get wealth and power. The fallen angels showed them how to extract purple dye from the seashell and make clothing out of it. Only royal people could wear purple, and Tiffany Blue was also their color. The fallen angels are here, and they have been here from the beginning. They make deals with certain people that vibrate in their lower chakras or lower vibrations.

August 09, 2023

I am here on this windy day and so grateful to be alive here. I was just meditating with the Holy Spirit and talking about nobody wanting me to wake up. That's the complete truth. I have been under a demonic force since I have been alive. They knew who I was before I ever did. I was put through so much trials and tribulations sometimes it feels did this shit really happened to me? Yes, it did, and I am so grateful that I am alive and woke to all this demonic influences, hexes, spell work, and witchcraft, sending in as fake lovers and friends to monitor me and cause to pull on and harvesting my energy. They have been energy harvesting me for many years. I guess they thought I would never wake up to who I am; well, surprise, I am alive and well, and I know exactly who I am and what's been happening to me.

I never even knew about *chosen* people. I knew about Moses, Jonah, but not me. I never thought of me being a descendant of the Most High, but I am. I am so grateful for all the tribulations, agony, and persecutions that I have been under because if this never happened to me, I couldn't tell you about the joy of God who sustained me during all my days in the wilderness. I am grateful to my enemies for elevating me to my best version of myself. Thank you very much.

I am still being watched. My neighbors watched me; they had a little truck parked by the dog park in which I walked to, and they were always home. I heard people walking in my attic all the time. I prayed they will be exposed soon by authorities. I'm not sure if they're CIA, Freemason, eastern stars, luciferins, satanic worshippers, witches, warlocks, fallen angels, demonic spirits, or demons.

One thing I know for sure is that God, the all-seeing eye, hears all, sees all, and knows all. So whatever anybody thinks they are getting away with, I leave all to the Most High his vengeance. I don't go for revenge; I leave it to God. I just pray and rebuke and pray and rebuke, sending these demonic forces back *to the* ring of fire where they belong, amen.

September 07, 2023

Hi, I'm back. I have been writing in my journal and not typing. It seems like every time I want to work on my novel, I felt bored and bored with my story, like there's a blockage. It was weird, and every time I wanted to focus on my Father's work, there would be a feeling like not wanting to do it. It's kind of weird that it continues to happen on a daily basis. I am aware of what they are doing. I am fighting through this spiritual warfare. Amen, amen.

September 08, 2023

Okay, I am back today; it is a beautiful day. I have been writing down my daily routines and journaling. I have been under spiritual attacks for fifty years, and these last six months, it's been getting better. I feel a little lighter. Sometimes, I cry because of the trauma. It happens. I have prayed more, talked to Spirit more, taken spiritual baths, and meditated. I feel this last year, I have prayed more and talked to the Holy Spirit all the time. He's all around me, us. I'm forgiving myself, family, and friends. Although no one has confessed to what they have done against me, I forgive them and really thank them for helping me to finally wake the hell up.

I can't believe that I am fifty-three. Like wow. I'm glad and grateful for my life especially my shadow life. My shadow self is here with me and always with me because that is the way God intended it to be. This is the self-will he gave us. I feel like I have learned those karmic lessons and I have released everything that no longer serves my higher good to the divine.

When I woke up and my life was in pain, anguish, despair, alone, depressed over and over again, I looked up to the sky to God and cried from my heart *why* this is happening to me. That's when the Holy Spirit touched my life and me, and I felt an overwhelming warm feeling all over my body. It was supernatural, and I knew God was there with me and he was always with me; I just didn't know.

September 16, 2023

Hello, here I am. It's Saturday and a beautiful day. I've been feeling as if something is going to happen soon; I don't know what, but I feel it in my soul. I am very grateful for how God is making me feel. I feel secure, safe, *and* loved.

I've been by myself without anyone living with me for the last five months, maybe three months. Christina moved out shortly after Emmanuel and is living with her boyfriend, Edwin. I am very grateful that she is such a good mother. We sometimes have issues, but I am so proud of how she is turning into a great mom. I pray she will respect me and love me again.

September 22, 2023

It's 7:50 p.m., and I have been doing a lot of journaling, writing, not typing. I feel something is going to happen.

September 28, 2023

I have been journaling in my notepad every day. I'm learning everyday about spiritual warfare.

October 04, 2023, 11:16 a.m.

Today is Wednesday, and I have been getting a lot of messages on things that I hear. I have been studying a lot of tarot, spiritual warfare, prayer warfare, and prophetess. I am very grateful for all the love my Creator has for me and always did. I just didn't know that because I didn't even love myself like my Creator intended me to. I pretty much had no knowledge of spiritual warfare. It feels like my whole life, I have had my eyes blinded, folded for fifty-three years since I was born. It's weird to think that now because of how much information is being downloaded and so many synchroneities. It's absolutely amazing to know that there is another power around me that is for me and loves me. I am by myself, and this is highly unusual for me.

My life has always been programmed to look for validation from others to like me or that I am the right pick. When I don't get picked, it used to make me go crazy in the head and very depressed, and I spiral down into a lot of addictions that I didn't need in my life. I am so grateful for my Creator to enlighten me and for *waking me up*. I am a star seed and am a child of God the Creator, and I am here to help divine beings awaken to their divinity and the collective. All my experiences in my life are a true testimony of the amount of spiritual warfare that has been done on a person that was supposed to be *dead* by now. My Creator God, King of the universe says, "*Nah, not today. Amen.*"

October 05, 2023

It is raining today, and I have the maintenance people here looking at my ceiling where it is leaking. It's bad; it's all coming down on the corner of the room all the way down. I do not want to stay here with mold in the apartment. It was weird for the first two nights; it was water coming down from the ceiling, and I had to clean it with a mop and put a bucket down. I called the apartment manager to tell her about it, and she told me to take a video. Now this was two nights ago.

Now last night, around 4:00 a.m., the alarms in the apartment started going off. The fire department had to come and turn it off. Me and Ladybug was outside in my car because it was hurting her ears. The leak was getting worse, and it's not stopping raining. I suggested to the manager to put a tarp over the leak until it stopped raining because it was getting worse. Wow, I guess, God, I might be moving? Who knows? Only God is the author of my life. Amen. I love God so much that whatever he wants, I will obey. He has saved my life so many times. I could not even exist without him.

I'm here in my apartment typing, thinking how beautiful our Creator is, how much love he has for us. I am so grateful for everything he has been doing in my life, and I will always honor and obey him. I can do anything with him in my life.

Thank you for purchasing my book and hearing my testimony. I will be honored to help people to come to their purpose in life and to come to God our Creator, Jesus Christ. Amen. Peace.

Spiritual natural events that happened in my life before my awakening , after and during. A lot of people will say oh it's just a coincidence. I used to feel like that too but since my spiritual awakening and having a personal relationship with the Holy Spirit my Creator I know different. Praise God for whom all blessings flow.

This is a continuation from my first part of the book explaining my awakening and how God spoke with me. He was always with me, but I didn't realize that I am part of this beautiful new earth that is coming. Last night God woke me up and I could hear him say Tribe of Benjamin and the planet Neptune. I do know that Neptune is the 8th planet from us and 2024 is the year of 8. Amen thank you Jesus

I just recently found out that the house I lived in for 18 years that someone had died in it. I don't know how they died if it was murder or natural. I asked my mom recently and she said yes and acted as if I should have already known? I'm like what I told her that I would never have moved in there if I knew that. Then she got up from the chair at the kitchen table and started talking with my oldest daughter Meghan in the kitchen. Wow ... so creepy.

My youngest daughter Christina was born in Conroe, Texas. She came straight from the hospital to this house. When she was around 1 to ½ years old she told me mom look and pointed at the ceiling asking me momma who is that man? I looked and saw nothing.... My daughter could see the spirit. Or a spirit.... Maybe she saw angels too.....

I'm not saying to anyone that I am any better than the next person. My journey of this life so far has brought me to here and I am willing to share my experiences with the world. I always felt that I had something better for my life. That there is something of greatness to my spirit, soul. This is my journey, and I know that the population of humankind can relate to experiences like I have had in my life. I just always felt that this was life, and you got to take those bad apples. But for how long? This is not the way god wants me to live my life. Feeling oppressed, confused, and fearful.

Last year I saw a wheel and it was purple. And it was in my room just hovering in my room. It was awesome to see this. Thank you, God.

Part II Before my Awakening

Spiritual natural events that happened in my life before my awakening. A lot of people will say oh it's just a coincidence. I used to feel like that too but since my spiritual awakening and having a personal relationship with the Holy Spirit my Creator I know different. Praise God for whom all blessings flow.

This is a continuation from my first part of the book explaining my awakening and how God spoke with me. He has always been with me, but I didn't realize that I am part of this beautiful new earth that is coming. Last night God woke me up and I could hear him say Tribe of Benjamin and the planet Neptune. I do know that Neptune is the 8th planet from us and 2024 is the year of 8. Amen thank you Jesus

I just recently found out that the house I lived in for 18 years that someone had died in it. I don't know how they died if it was murder or natural. I asked my mom recently and she said yes and acted as if I should have already known? I'm like what I told her that I would never have moved in there if I knew that. Then she got up from the chair at the kitchen table and started talking with my oldest daughter Meghan in the kitchen. Wow … so creepy.

My youngest daughter Christina was born in Conroe, Texas. She came straight from the hospital to this house. When she was around 1 to ½ years old she told me mom look and pointed at the ceiling asking me momma who is that man? I looked and saw nothing…. My daughter could see the spirit. Or a spirit…. Maybe she saw angels too….

I'm not saying to anyone that I am any better than the next person. My journey of this life so far has brought me to here and I am willing to share my experiences with the world. I always felt that I had something better for my life. That there is something of greatness to my spirit, soul. This is my journey, and I know that the population of humankind can relate to experiences like I have had in my life. I just always felt that this was life and you got to take those bad apples. But for how long? This is not the way god wants me to live my life. Feeling oppressed, confused, and fearful.

Last year I saw a wheel and it was purple. And it was in my room just hovering in my room. It was awesome to see this. Thank you, God.

This part of my story is before my Awakening and the trials and tribulations that I went through. I know that it is important to share these trials and tribulations of my life because this is what made me who I am today and what I discover every day of my life.

When I was at an incredibly youthful age I can remember having a very normal childhood, at least in my eyes it seemed normal. I grew up in the seventies before any electronics, cell phones, internet etc. If someone called your house, you were not home and that was about it. You sometimes would hear about receiving a phone call if you were lucky. There were a lot less distractions with electronics. We of course had television. Programming us on sesame street, Mr. Rogers neighborhood etc. I can also remember watching a lot of fantasy shows, sorcery, clash of the titans, bewitched, wizard of oz, star trek, sorcery movies, and biblical movies really touched me. It was so amazing to watch. Needless to say, I loved movies.

I was a very outdoors child. I can remember my mom yelling my name in the neighborhood when it was getting dark to come home. I could hear her and hop on my bike and take off and go home.

It was a simpler life without all the electronics I would say. If we had questions about something as a kid I would ask my father, and then look it up in the Encyclopedia to find out what the answers were. Just to think about that now is crazy to me. You used to see an Encyclopedia set in all homes back in that era.

When I was in the 5 th grade, I was introduced to shoplifting. I knew it was wrong because of the Ten Commandments but I was tempted to steal barbie dolls at a Store like target or Walmart when I was younger, I cannot recall the store. Me and two other little girl friends would walk in the store with 1 bag and fill it full of barbies and barbie clothes and we would take turn walking out of the store between us 3. We did this for several months and one day it was my turn and when I walked out of the store, I felt a hand on my shoulder, and it was a cop that was dressed in regular clothing and he stopped me. I looked at my other two friends and they kept going. He took me upstairs inside the store, where the mirrors are. He read me my rights and I started crying. I told on the other girls. My dad was terribly upset with me and my brother was really gas lighting me making me feel so bad. I can say that it really did an effect on me in life. I still did some shoplifting after that incident later in life during my addiction but not very often.

I was very athletic in gymnastics. I could do round off back handsprings, front handsprings, round off back flips, and every split you could think off. I could do back walker overs and front walk overs on the balanced beams and was incredibly good at swimming.

I can remember beautiful memories living in Gulf breeze walking a few blocks to the beach and staying out there for hours and hours. It was like I was in another world. It was so beautiful.

Times started changing with my parents and they separated. My father moved to Texas, and I stayed with my mom in Pensacola, Florida.

I was in the sixth grade and started skating a lot in Florida. I would go to the skating rink every Friday night and stay from 7 to 12. I had my own skates and would meet up with friends from school and do the shuffle on skates around the rink. It was a good time. Although my mom was dating someone else I did not like. I would visit my dad on holiday and then come back to live with my mom. I did not like the separation from my dad. I guess you can say I was daddy's little girl. We were very close. I decided after doing this for several years in the 8th grade I decided to live with my dad. It was a definite culture change from Pensacola Florida to Conroe Texas. After about a year living with my dad. My dad went to Florida and told my mom either came back with me now or we are getting a divorce. She came back with my dad, and they did not divorce. My family was now together. My brother had joined the Army. My sister was pregnant when she moved here with my mom. Not much longer my nephew was born. I was in the 9th grade now. School was good getting to know more people because now I was in high school. I was a regular girl, volleyball team, pep squad, average grades good girl. In the tenth grade I started to notice boys and going to concerts. I really enjoyed going to concerts. I loved the energy and how I felt. I was into rock and roll, Ozzy Osburne, Metallica, acdc, judas priest and all those 70s, 80s bands. I was a rock and roller. When I was 14 years old went to the Texas jam in Mesquite Texas and stayed the night in a hotel with 2 of my high school friends with her older sister and boyfriend. I was a free spirit. My dad use to tell me all the time that I was born in the wrong era. I really can see that now. During my 10th grade I met my boyfriend. I'm going to call him high school boyfriend to leave names out. I was here thinking of how I met him. Honestly, I cannot even remember how I met him. He was not in high school he had dropped out and was working with his dad with their air conditioning business. I was so young and very naive. You know, like most of us was when we were young. I was head over heels in love and was having a lot of sex with him. I never got the concept of what true love was. I just thought it was having sex. Actually, I got my first organism, and I thought that was what love was. Is when you have an organism from another person you are having sex was love. I didn't know much or anything about sex, love, relationships, boyfriends, etc. The high school boyfriend introduced me also to hard drugs. This was in the year 1986. This is when crack cocaine hits the streets. I experimented with crystal meth, marijuana, acid, mushrooms, speed, downers, cocaine and extasy. I experimented with him. I'm not blaming anyone for my choices in those areas or anything. This is what happened to me. He introduced me to crack cocaine. We were at his older sister's apartment where we used to hang out on the weekends. I was 16 and he was 18. A neighbor man came over and they were in the kitchen. I didn't know what they were doing but when I walked in there were like 10 rocks on the countertop and they were smoking it. I had never seen it before didn't know anything about it. I tried it and immediately went to the living room and was absolutely terrified and hated it. My boyfriend stayed in this kitchen all night smoking. I felt rejected, abandoned like wow he is totally ignoring me because I don't want to smoke that. So, the next weekend came around and we were at his sister's apartment and here comes the neighbor and they are in the kitchen again. I was getting upset because he was not spending any time with me. So, I went in the kitchen thinking well shit I might as well try it again maybe I did something wrong. After that second try, that was it. The monkey was on my back. I went into another world. This led to me spiraling during my 11th and 12 grade in high school. It took me to bad places and had me out sometimes all night. During my 12 th grade my father asked me one day hey Yvette come take a ride with me. He knew something was wrong with me. I can remember coming home from doing drugs and I would have to walk past his bedroom to get to my bedroom and he would hear me and say he Yvette and I would walk over there. He would tell me that if there is something I want to talk about to him that he is always there. I couldn't tell him but he knew. It was like a weird telepathic communication, but of course when you have children you can always tell if something is bothering your child. My dad asked me to take a ride with him on the weekend and he wanted to show me something. I went with him, and he took me to a Rehab. I didn't know what it was, we drove up to this building and there was a lady standing outside waving. We got out and she introduced herself and we all went inside. We walked around and it was an Inpatient Rehabilitation Drugs, alcohol, bipolar, sexual abuse etc. It was a high-end one. We left and I promised my dad that I would not do any more drugs. The next weekend I was there. It was an experience. I don't know if you have ever been a drug rehab before, but this was a very expensive one, but it was a program that we had to participate in. It was very eye opening. During my stay there was a female resident my age 17 that got a key from the cook and opened one of the doors to this rehab. During the night we all got pulled out of our rooms to the day room and was told that one of the residents that was in there escaped but while crossing the freeway got hit and torn to pieces all over the highway. It was a terrible accident. After leaving this rehab and then I went and graduated high school. I was the first one in my family to walk across the field to receive their high school diploma. I was very grateful and felt great because I was drug free.

I went to a junior college, but I really didn't want to go so I went for a semester. My dad paid for it he basically made me go. I only stayed for a semester. I wanted to be free from institutions, schools, or anything that was telling me what to do. I felt free when I was 18 and had my whole life to look forward to. That high school boyfriend moved away, and I finally got over him. I ended up getting a job at the Texas Department of Corrections in Huntsville, Texas. It was at the BOT warehouse. I was basically processing inmate's folders when they came to prison. Putting them together, visitors list, medical, psychological interviews I dictated. It was a good job and I met a girl we became best friends. She was going through a divorce, and I was getting over that boyfriend. We did a lot of drinking together needless to say I was 19 turning 20 at this time. We had a lot of fun and a lot of drinking and taking acid, going to concerts and meeting boys. We were at the Lake Conroe partying one day and someone gave me a pain pill and I was drinking liquor and beer. I was mixing which is never a good combination. I was invited to a party in town by a male friend. I had a couple of guy friends with me, and one was African American. We went to the party and the guy who invited got upset because I brought my friends, and he didn't like the African American because of his skin color and kicked me out of the party. We left but I was totally drunk and on that pain pill. I was very upset and listening to my Metallica loud and head banging while driving and ran into a cement culvert. They had to get the jaws of life out to get me and my friends out. I was 4 points of dying from alcoholism. I broke my ankle and bone popped out of my ankle. They had to wait for my level of alcohol to go down before they operated on me. My friends suffered injuries as a passenger had half of his ear taken off which had to get fixed and the other had a lot of cuts and bruises. Thank god none of us lost out life's. It was a definite wake up call for me. The doctor came to see me in the hospital room the next day and chastised me stating this is what I get for drinking and driving. I received 2 screws in my ankle. I no longer had a car so I stayed with the girl I meet at TDCJ to go back and forth to work since I no longer had a car. We continued to drink a lot while I was healing, and my ankle never healed properly. When I got my cast off my ankle and started walking on it I ended up breaking the screws in my ankle and got a bone infection in my ankle. I had to get a n iv put in my chest and have a iv drip with a home nurse coming to my house twice a week for 6 weeks to get rid of the infection in my bone so I can have surgery where they had to scrape the infection off of my bone on my ankle. I had to wait several months and have another surgery with them taking a piece of my bone out of my hips and fuse it to my ankle with 6 screws 1 ½ inch long putting my ankle back together again. I was on crutches for 2 years and 3 surgeries. It was definitely a life changing event in my life. I had to learn how to walk again after all these surgeries. I was scared to put any weight on it because what had happened to me prior. During this time, I was still going out I turned 21 and started going to the bars with my crutches. I met my Meghan's dad in a bar. I was on crutches, and we hooked up. I told me I had a problem with cocaine and all I do is drink and smoke weed but I don't do anything else. After a few months of dating, I found out that Meghan's dad was shooting up cocaine. At this time, I had already fallen in love. I asked him to promise too never do it again. I kept catching him doing it. After so many times I just started joining in on snorting cocaine. Also found out that my good friend from work that I lived with was having sex with him and I was devasted. I couldn't believe it. I ended up taking Meghan's dad back but was still upset with her. All my friends were like you forgave him why not her? So, I forgave her. She was always around getting in the middle of our relationship. We use go to the tattoo place in Houston called DAGOS and bring like a case of beer and watch people get tattoos and shoot pool. I eventually got one and it was a peace sign, but I got in on my bikini line because I didn't want my parents to see it. She started getting big wizards on her back. It was like it opened a can of worms on her. She became obsessed with tattoos. I got another one of marijuana leaf on it because I didn't want her to get what I was going to get and I loved to smoke weed. I got it with my initials hers and Meghan's dad. The tattoo artists put hers in between our initials and she use to bragged to him about it and saying she will always be between us. Looking back on it, that's pretty weird. She always love to be around us and just pop up at my apartment all the time unannounced.

I also got pregnant during this time. I was partying a lot, and my parents convinced me to get an abortion. I remember my girlfriend took me. It's weird but I remember going and coming out of there. When I sit here and think about it, it is kind of like a blur for me. I don't know if that is how my subconscious or conscience self-took it. I have prayed to my father God to forgive me, and he has. This happened over 30 years ago.

She got tickets for the front row to the Metallica Black album concert in Houston at the summit arena in 1991. She invited me to go and so I went. Before we went to the concert stopped to see Meghan's dad and did some crystal meth. On our way to the summit, it was raining and really stormy weather at night. Right when we were getting out of Montgomery County, she got a blow out on her car and we did 2 360's in the car and bumped the freeway wall and did 2 more 360's going the other way. It was so surreal. While we were spinning, I can remember holding her hang and praying to god. Needless to say, we ended up on the side of the freeway okay. All we had was a blow out. We got out of the car to get help, and someone stopped and helped us put a spare tire on the car. She looked at me and said do you still want to go to the concert. I said HELL YES. We took off. The Methamphine we did was really feeling strong in my body and my hair was moving all around on my scalp. We got to the summit and parked the car. We went straight inside and bought a T-shirt and walked to the floor. They had security there and the concert had just started. I asked the lady at the ticket booth if anyone was going to take us to our front row seats she said you are on your own now. People were head banging and there was a big mosh pit. We were so close to the stage. As we were walking on the floor, we got separated I got bashed and fell down and lost my friend. People were everywhere going crazy, running, bumping, screaming just everything, pushing. I got angry and found my friend and told her we are going to get out seats. I was ready to fight. I pushed my way up there. There were groupies were are seats were and I told them to get the hell out. Really everyone was standing. They left and, as you know, chairs were being held over our heads. They were all tied together but were getting stacked in front of us. I airheaded butted so hard. We were so close. They had a lot of explosions with fire. I could smell my hair getting burned. It was crazy.

After this concert things were pretty crazy in my life. I was working and living with Meghan's dad in an apartment. We were doing a lot of drinking and drugging, partying. At this time, we were still functioning as to working a job and paying rent, bills etc. Of course, things didn't last like that but for a short time, a few years. The drugs go worse, and we ended up moving around a lot. Living with different friends. We would stay for a few months and leave and go somewhere else. My mom said I lived like a gypsy. I guess I did.

The last place we lived at was with a single woman. She was like cool and always did drugs and had her own house. While we were living there, I was getting tired of this life. I felt as though I didn't fit in no matter what. One night my x was in the other room playing cards with some people. I was lying on the bed in our bedroom that we were renting. I could hear them talking and stuff like that. Then I looked up at the ceiling and saw 7 Angels with wings, and white clothing flying over me. Like they were hovering over me. It scared me and I immediately packed up all my belongings in my car and left there and drove home immediately. I got to my parents' house, and I slept for 2 days. I know what I saw.

Meghan's dad came to my parents' house and begged and asked me to go with him to Louisiana and he would change. He told me he loved me and wanted me to be with him. I fell for it. My dad warned me not to go or he would disown me. I went in my car with my things and him and moved to Louisiana.

It only took 1 week, and we were fighting, and I loaded up my car with my clothes and was gonna leave. He stopped me and popped the hood and tore out a piece of a wire and broke my car. He was getting unemployment that was gonna take another 2 weeks. The part for my car to get ordered was not something you can get at the dealership. It had to be ordered. I got a job at 7 eleven up the street where I could walk to. After I got the part for my car, I got a better job.

I went to the local free clinic to check to see if I was pregnant because I skipped a period. I went there and they told me no. I thought I wasn't pregnant and continued partying living life. I got arrested downtown Lafayette due to drunk driving. I had a court appointed lawyer. After I got out, I found out I was pregnant with Meghan. I was 4 months pregnant. The court appointed lawyer told me I have two options either stay in Louisiana and get on probation or leave Louisiana and go back to Texas and never come back. I did the second one and we hauled ass to Texas. We started hanging out with the wrong people and I did get high while pregnant. Meghan's dad got 10 ounces of cocaine fronted to him. He took off. I was 8 to 9 months pregnant freaking out because everybody was hiding him out in hotels not telling me where he was. I finally went to Holiday Inn and found him. He was so high I saw the ounces in bags on the bathroom counter, needles, crack. It was so surreal. His eyes were huge, and I told him let's give this back to the dealer. At this time, I heard a knock on the door, and it was the police. He jumped up and grabbed the bags of cocaine and started ripping them up and shoving them down the toilet to flush. The police gathered him and what evidence was left, and the ambulance came to pick him up because he was saying it's all over now and saying he was seeing little green people. I went to my friend's house to gather his stuff up. Then all a sudden there he was at the back door. I couldn't believe it. The police let him go. I had Meghan on 03-07-1994. I had her naturally. The nurse wouldn't give me a epidural because I was already dilated at 4 when I went to the hospital. At least this is what she told me and if she gave me the epidural it would slow down the baby coming. I had her natural. I wanted to say also this is when I found out I was RH-. I had to get this shot when I was around 6 to 7 months pregnant. They really didn't tell me anything about it just saying I need to get this for the baby to survive. It's weird but I never thought to investigate what RH- was at that time. I had a baby girl named Meghan. She was so beautiful, and I was so happy. I would always hold her and my x in-laws use to tell me you need to put her down some. Which I did but I was so amazed. I would say that Jesus sent me a angel from heaven to be with me. Not too much longer after that her father was locked up. He was away for about a year. He paroled to Surf side beach. Meghan and I moved to be with him on a little trailer on the beach. We tried to make it work but we started doing drugs down there and it spiraled out of control. We moved back to our hometown and go caught leaving a dope house and he got arrested. I was so scared that I kept out for several more days because I was so ashamed that this had happened, and I knew his parents and mine were pissed. I didn't want to face reality. I noticed a lot in my life that I was a escapism I would always escape to drugs when things were going bad and it got to where if things would go good. I was lost. I went to several rehabs off and on in my life. I went to junior college for a little time. Eventually I got a little customer service job. Later her father got released and we tried to make it work one more time, but we were both addicts and couldn't do it. He eventually found someone else when Meghan was about 3 years old. During this time, I was working but also using. He came to my parent's house one day and got Meghan and hid her out. His parents wouldn't tell me where they were. I called the police, and the police told me that since were haven't gone to court yet for conservatorship that since he is the father he has every legal right. I would have to go to court. That could take months. I was so upset. Instead of doing the right thing I started really going into my addiction. I eventually got summoned in my addiction for court for my daughter and didn't even go because I was in my addiction. I was ashamed. During these days I would stay gone for days at a time in my addiction and then drive home. Sometimes I wouldn't even remember driving home. I remember leaving the place I was at but I would black out and then wake up when the car was going up the bumpy dirt road going to my parents house. This happened to me at least 20 or more times. I didn't know that there was something powerful around me that I didn't know. I just ignored all the signs of the universe. I was in the world and my addictions. I was going in and out of rehabs during this time. I was so ashamed that I lost the custody of my kid and I was a addict. I had nothing going on in my life. I felt ashamed to even pray to go for help. I was out there in my addictions, prostitution, drugs, the elements of that life. I experienced traumatic things that changed my whole life, and I felt numb. The one thing that I can say was I did have hope that this life would get better. I always had a inner knowing deep down inside that my life was not this life. I cried out to God one night in my addiction asking for God to help me. It wasn't that much longer that night than I got arrested. I believe that is what I deserved, although I wasn't happy. I never really got into this kind of situation before. I ended up getting probation. I failed a UA not that much longer after probation. I ended up getting arrested. While I was in county, A secret indictment came through. The indictment stated they had me on camera selling to undercover. I never seen the tape though. I ended up getting 2 years of State Jail. I was devasted. My father in court ran out of the court room very upset. He wrote to me stating he hired a lawyer. He was very upset and felt that was a very unjust sentence. Like I was being made a example. While I was in state prison I told my bunk mate about it and she said no one every gets to go back to court after there sentence. So I learned to keep my mouth shut about anything that had to do with me. About 4 to 6 weeks later I got a ATW back to court and was before the same judge. He changed my sentence to 4-to-6-month SAFEP REHABILATION and then 3 years shock probation. I completed the 4 to 6 MTh rehab and went to downtown Houston, a house for 90 days and moved back home.

I got a local job at the TAX office and my shock probation officer used to come visit me during work. I did relapse and was devasted. I know that judge told me he would give me 3 years with no good time if I messed up. I was lost in my addiction. Also, during this time, I got an infection on my finger. It swells up and it looks nasty. I let someone pop it and it got an infection. I got gangrene on my thumb and was now full back in my addiction. I was totally scared, confused and LOST. I met someone during this time that talked to me and told me he would take me back home to my parents. To call the Probation and tell them that I was going to a rehab. So, this is what I did. I went to a free place for women in Pasadena Texas. I had to go and get my finger looked at. This is where they had to take a piece of the tip of my bone off my thumb cut off and stitch it back up. I was on so many antibiotics it was unreal. This was probably the second encounter of death in my life during my addiction that I was physically damaged, and emotionally drained. I was sober when I was at this woman's house. My finger finally healed up. That was supposed to be a reminder of what happened during my last relapse. I stayed sober for around 2 years. My daughter was now living with my mom. I got a lawyer and proceeded to get full custody of Meghan also during this time. I was driving back and forth spending every weekend with my daughter Meghan. I got me an apartment and was feeling good about my sobriety, working, things looked up for me finally.

This was during the time of 911 happened when I was in my apartment. I had to call the police the same day 9/11 happened because my car had gotten broken into at the apartments I was living at. It was so surreal. They never found the person and my car was broken into two more times when I was living in Pasadena. I met my second child's father at the Rehab before I moved into my apartment. We didn't really hit it off at first because he was with someone. He made me believe his lies to be truths. I see that now. It was really a story of his hardships, and I fell for it and told me he just got released from prison for doing 8 years for a drug case. I fell for it. He was exotic looking and was dark, built, he didn't have a 6 pack he had a 8 pack. I had never been with a man that looked like that. So, I fell really hard. We got together. I got pregnant and he moved in with me. I was still getting my daughter from my hometown every weekend and bringing her back to stay the weekend. She didn't like him. I should have been more observant and listened to her. You know your kids will tell you something about someone before you can ever see them or it. I just didn't see it like that. I wanted them to get a long so bad. I had Emily which I had to get another Rhogam shot because I am Rh-negative. She came out and was the most beautiful baby and I was so happy and felt like I have a family. We stayed in Pasadena until Emily was around 4 or 5 years old. I got approved for a new KB Home and put down the 2000.00. We picked out our house. During this time Emilys dad was at the first stages of molesting Meghan and I didn't know about it. My dad was alive at this time, and he wanted me to move back close to him. I don't know why but he did not want me to move into that new home. He found a home about 5 miles from where he lives. It was a double wide mobile home on 1 ½ acres. This was not what I was anticipating considering I was waiting for my new 2 story home to be built. The home my dad found is in my hometown where I had been in and out of my addictions and graduated high school at. Listen I know all about my hometown and all the hoods, spots, places, drugs, you get my drift. I had been sober while I was living in Pasadena, Texas. Now everybody wanted me to move back to my hometown and give up the 2000.00 down payment and contract on my new home I already signed paperwork on and go live back there. I was not happy. I didn't like this idea. I didn't know why my dad was adamant to want me to move back closer to him. I don't know if he knew something that I didn't. We were very close. It was like a telekinetic relationship. He could always know in my voice if something was wrong on the phone. Or he could just sense my energy. When you have children, you can sense when something is going on with them if they are in tune with you. I know that to be true. I wish I had been more at tune with Meghan like my dad was, at that time. I ended up relapsing in Pasadena before I moved. It was awful. I ended up going on a Benger several weeks when we first got there. It was terrible. I could remember being up for like 5 days and I was at a person's house using and knowing I want to come home. I didn't even have enough gas to get there. He gave me 5.00 to put in my gas to go home. I put it in and took off on the freeway and all the sudden I was screaming and shaking my self to wake up. I fell asleep on the freeway, and I woke up to it felt like someone was shaking me. I was in some neighborhood screaming because I didn't know where I was or what had happened to me. I was close to my mother's house and drove there around 3 am. I knocked on the door and told my mom what happened. We got on our knees right there holding hands and thanking God that he protected and saved my life. It's weird to think about that now but I fell asleep a lot when I was driving home from drugging for days. I know that there is something around me protecting me. Amen

I ended up getting another case. While I was in jail I got offered drug court. I took it. Also, CPS had been called on me. Emilys dad got into a accident and totaled his bran new work truck that was in my name bran new from the Chevrolet dealership. My daughter Emily was in the truck in the accident and survived. She's got scars on her leg from that accident as a child. I completed drug court and got pregnant again and another Rhogam shot was administered. Emilys dad and I were not getting a long very good at this time. I had a new girl named Christina. She was so beautiful blonde hair blue eyes. After she was 4 months I got a job at a Urology Office. I was a Patient Service Representative for 5 years. I was also going to school online with DeVry University. Emilys dad stayed home. I didn't know if I said but he gets SSI because he is legally blind. So, he gets checks every month. So, he stayed home baby sitting Christina. He would help with getting the girls on the bus every morning and be there and be there when they would get off the bus. I worked full time and went to school online at night. I was very busy. I felt happy. There was a feeling I was getting because Emilys dad was always in Meghan's room playing video games with her. I also noticed she was never getting phone calls or going out. He would tell me she's helping with her little sisters, at least she's not like how you were out in the streets and doing drugs. It was so much manipulation looking back at it all now. One night I went in Meghan's room and closed the door and asked her if there was something going on between them and she said no. I also asked him and he said I am her friend. Her father is absent and has nothing to do with her. I'm not trying to be her father, dad, but her friend. He told me is that how I want him to be. He switched it around as if I was so disgusting to even think that way about him. He was trying to be her friend since her dad had nothing to do with her. So much manipulation. I believed them continued on with my life there working, going to school, and being a mother to my children.

It was around 2010 when my dad started falling a lot. I got a phone call early one morning from my mom saying that my dad is not breathing. I asked her did you call 911 and she said no she called me. I told her to call 911 and I headed to her house. I got there and my dad was lying there super cold. I yelled at him, and he took a breath. About that time the EMS was there and heard his heartbeat barely and they took him to the ER. The doctor told me that he had a heart attack and they had to bring him back to life. It was terrible.

My father was the only one I felt in my life that ever really loved me with all my faults. He never judged me but always lifted my spirits like my cheerleader in my corner. Not to much later he then got diagnosed with ALS. I never heard of it. I started diving into that disease wanting to know what it was. I was devasted. It states once you're diagnosed that you have about 2 years to live. I would go to work and then go visit my dad after work to see him. He was having home health care nurses coming to the house. He had a trac to and could no longer eat solid foods. He couldn't talk but I could understand everything he was saying. My mother and brother couldn't believe how I could understand. My dad would tell me things that would happen to him during the day that he didn't like. My brother and mother were with him every day while I was working. I was like a robot. I had a mental break down at my house one day and was crying so hard on my child's bed because I knew that he was soon to die. I was hyper ventilating and just couldn't stop crying. Then all a sudden I felt this electrical charge go up my spine and it was the weirdest thing I ever felt. I started having like these little ticks of nervous movements in my body. I guess you could say I was having a nervous mental breakdown. I ended up leaving working on FMLA. I was very depressed. One day I was telling my EX that I wanted to go and do something fun and get out of the house and he refused. He didn't want to go anywhere. I felt like I needed to and I left and went back to my drugging ways. I started using it again while my dad was dying, I would go see him and crying it was a mess. When I would go home my EX would tell me that I didn't belong there anymore. When I went to see my dad before he died. My mom wouldn't let me go in the house to see him right before he died. It was very terrible. I was again lost and by myself. I had been out using it to cope with my dad slowly dying and my whole family was against me. I was probably out for about 5 days and I went home one night and my EX was there and tell my kids to stay away from me that I was a monster. I took a shower and laid down and he told me he was going to lay down on the floor of Meghan's room. We were arguing and he said he was scared I was going to do something to him. I went to sleep for a little while and got up and my daughter Emily was playing

ROBLOX and told me that when I was away from the house that Dad would sleep with Meghan and Christina. Right then I went to her bedroom, and he was lying on the floor and I told him to get out of her room. He told me no; I told him again. He got up and started to strangle me around my neck. I couldn't breathe. He was choking me out. Meghan jumped off her bed and told me to stop it and he did. I ran to my bedroom and called 911. The police came and he was out there talking to them telling them I was on drugs, and I was not a good mother etc. They knocked on the door and wanted to talk to me because I was the one who called them. They looked at my neck and could see the fingerprints of where he was strangling me. They arrested him. This is when I found out that my EX had been molesting my child for several years. She was now 18 and completely brainwashed to believe she was in love with him. She had told me later in life that she felt so guilty and told him this and he told her that if she told on him that she would be frowned upon as being the one that has been having sex with her mother's boyfriend. He told her that I was the crown, and she was the jewel that he was slowly picking off my crown. Pretty sadistic that this man was brain washing and manipulating my daughter against me undercover for years. I believe he is a warlock he has a star with a circle branded on the inside of his arm. He told me when we first met that it was a gang affiliation, I believe it to be more sinister than that. He was arrested and I put a restraining order against him. He could not come on my property and also he had to leave the state of Texas. My daughter was 18 when he got arrested and she did not want to file charges against him at the time. My father died on October 28, 2012 with ALS. I went down a deep depression and more drugs. I was getting a quarter of a cocaine almost every day. I would sit up and smoke and cry because of what happened to my daughter, what my EX had been doing for years and my father dying. I wanted to die. In those dark night god said no you have small children that need you. I started believing again slowly in myself. I met a new guy who was bringing me drugs to my house. I didn't want to go back in the hood looking for drugs and someone sees me. I was in fear, depression, and sadness. I was mourning my family who had been torn apart. This is the time I kept waking up at

3:33am. I loved God Jesus Christ, but I was so ashamed of my life I felt like I was not good enough to even dare ask anything from God. This is just how I used to think. I would pray every night though. I didn't put it together why I was woke up at 3:33am. Also, I started do more and more drugs behind the scenes. I guess I was a someone functioning addict to a certain extinct. I would no longer stay gone for long periods of time now that my EX was gone and I found out about sexual abuse. Meghan and I were pretty rocky during these times. She had a lot of anger and shame about what happened. I told her it's not her fault she was just a child. He was the adult and new better. Our relationship now is remarkable. We have overcome a lot since then. Not perfect but more open and honest. My sister passed away from breast cancer in 2016. It was so sad. She was a very kindred spirit. I wish I had been more aware of spiritual warfare back then like I am now or getting there.

I was cleaning my house in the spring of 2018 and I cleaning the windows and under neath the carpet the cleaning supply was running down the window, so I was cleaning up under the carpet and found teeth there. I said what the hell is this I found like 6 teeth around my window. I don't know who put that there, but someone did. Also, when I was at my address with my EX there was a brick house there and 2 little trailers. I believe in my heart and soul that secret societies and the government has been orchestrating my life since I was born. This is because of my blood. Since I moved from there the trailers have been gone. I have caught people following me, gangs stalking me online and sending in opps to follow and monitor me all the time. This is where I am going to stop because in the next part of my book I go into more detail of when I started waking up to who I really am. Who God told me that I truly am. I am learning everyday about myself and my creator. I just felt this also needed to be shared as my full testimony as I remember what happened during my life. This is true facts that happened to me. If God came save me and forgive me he can for give you and change your whole life and give you the peace that you desire to have in your life. I am a walking testimony of my trials and tribulations in this world that we live in Jesus christ is real our father God. Peace

About the Author

Yvette is very grateful for her life. She thanks God for waking her up to who she is. It brought her to her soul's purpose and got her closer to her Creator, God Jesus Christ. She thanks everyone for purchasing this book and giving her an opportunity to share her story. She knows it will help people who have been through spiritual warfare. All praises go to God for her beautiful life.